SELECTED POEMS

STEPHEN SPENDER

Selected Poems

FABER AND FABER
London · Boston

First published in 1965
by Faber and Faber Limited
3 Queen Square London W.C.1
Reprinted 1970, 1975 and 1979
Printed in Great Britain by
Whitstable Litho Ltd., Whitstable, Kent
All rights reserved

ISBN 0 571 06358 6

Contents

Introduction

In making a Collected Poems one feels — I don't know quite why — under an obligation to put in nearly everything.

Selecting poems is a happier situation. One can cut away all the things about which one is most doubtful. If one doubts what remains it is because one doubts oneself anyway.

I have only excluded from this selection about a half-dozen poems which I would want to add if I were to make a new *Collected Poems*.

Certain readers who may be familiar with my poems may wonder why there are a few alterations. I can only say that I do not rewrite poems in the sense of adding new material. But — apart from those occasions when something seems so inept that it cries out to be improved — I sometimes remember, when I look at a poem, what I had originally meant to say: and I have another shot at saying it.

I have decided only to add three poems which have not previously been published in volume form. *Subject: Object: Sentence*, '*Earth-treading stars that make dark heaven light*' and *One More New Botched Beginning* may provide comment on a good deal of what has gone before. Therefore there seems some point in adding them. For the rest, I have so many tentatively written unpublished poems, that to try to select from them now would upset the balance of this selection. In any case, probably it is a good idea that poems which are collected or selected should first have gone through the probationary period of appearing in a separate volume. For permission to reprint the newly collected poems, acknowledgements are due to *The New Yorker*, *The New York Book Review* and, in England, to the Arts Council.

S. S.

Part One
FIRST POEMS

Icarus

He will watch the hawk with an indifferent eye
  Or pitifully;
Nor on those eagles that so feared him, now
  Will strain his brow;
Weapons men use, stone, sling and strong-thewed bow
  He will not know.

This aristocrat, superb of all instinct,
  With death close linked
Had paced the enormous cloud, almost had won
  War on the sun;
Till now, like Icarus mid-ocean-drowned,
  Hands, wings, are found.

Not to You

Not to you I sighed. No, not a word.
We climbed together. Any feeling was
Formed with the hills. It was like trees' unheard
And monumental sign of country peace.

But next day, stumbling, panting up dark stairs,
Rushing in room and door flung wide, I knew.
Oh empty walls, book-carcases, blank chairs
All splintered in my head and cried for you.

Waiting

Acts passed beyond the boundary of mere wishing
Not privy looks, hedged words, at times you saw.
These, blundering, heart-surrendered troopers were
Small presents made, and waiting for the tram.
Then once you said: 'Waiting was very kind',
And looked surprised. Surprising for me, too,
Whose every movement had been missionary,
A pleading tongue unheard. I had not thought
That you, who nothing else saw, would see this.

So 'very kind' was merest overflow
Something I had not reckoned in myself,
A chance deserter from my force. When we touched hands,
I felt the whole rebel, feared mutiny
And turned away,
Thinking, if these were tricklings through a dam,
I must have love enough to run a factory on,
Or give a city power, or drive a train.

Trigorin

An 'I' can never be great man.
This known great one has weakness
To friends is most remarkable for weakness:
His ill-temper at meals, dislike of being contradicted,
His only real pleasure fishing in ponds,
His only real wish—forgetting.

To advance from friends to the composite self,
Central 'I' is surrounded by 'I eating',
'I loving', 'I angry', 'I excreting',
And the great 'I' planted in him
Has nothing to do with all these,

Can never claim its true place
Resting in the forehead, secure in his gaze.
The great 'I' is an unfortunate intruder
Quarrelling with 'I tiring' and 'I sleeping'
And all those other 'I's who long for 'We dying'.

Beethoven's Death Mask

I imagine him still with heavy brow.
Huge, black, with bent head and falling hair,
He ploughs the landscape. His face
Is this hanging mask transfigured,
This mask of death which the white lights make stare.

I see the thick hands clasped; the scare-crow coat;
The light strike upwards at the holes for eyes;
The beast squat in that mouth, whose opening is
The hollow opening of an organ pipe:
There the wind sings and the harsh longing cries.

He moves across my vision like a ship.
What else is iron but he? The fields divide
And, heaving, are changing waters of the sea.
He is prisoned, masked, shut off from Being.
Life, like a fountain, he sees leap — outside.

Yet, in that head there twists the roaring cloud
And coils, as in a shell, the roaring wave.
The damp leaves whisper; bending to the rain
The April rises in him, chokes his lungs
And climbs the torturing passage of his brain.

Then the drums move away, the Distance shows:
Now cloud-hid peaks are bared; the mystic One
Horizons haze, as the blue incense, heaven.
Peace, peace. . . . Then splitting skull and dream, there comes
Blotting our lights, the Trumpeter, the sun.

Rough

My parents kept me from children who were rough
Who threw words like stones and who wore torn clothes.
Their thighs showed through rags. They ran in the street
And climbed cliffs and stripped by the country streams.

I feared more than tigers their muscles like iron
Their jerking hands and their knees tight on my arms.
I feared the salt coarse pointing of those boys
Who copied my lisp behind me on the road.

They were lithe, they sprang out behind hedges
Like dogs to bark at my world. They threw mud
While I looked the other way, pretending to smile.
I longed to forgive them, but they never smiled.

What I Expected

What I expected, was
Thunder, fighting,
Long struggles with men
And climbing.
After continual straining
I should grow strong;
Then the rocks would shake,
And I rest long.

What I had not foreseen
Was the gradual day
Weakening the will
Leaking the brightness away,
The lack of good to touch,
The fading of body and soul
— Smoke before wind,
Corrupt, unsubstantial.

The wearing of Time,
And the watching of cripples pass
With limbs shaped like questions
In their odd twist,
The pulverous grief
Melting the bones with pity,
The sick falling from earth —
These, I could not foresee.

Expecting always
Some brightness to hold in trust,
Some final innocence
Exempt from dust,
That, hanging solid,
Would dangle through all,
Like the created poem,
Or faceted crystal.

Souvenir de Londres

My parents quarrel in the neighbour room:
'How did you sleep last night?' 'I woke at four
To hear the wind that sulks along the floor
Blowing up dust like ashes from the tomb.'

'I was awake at three.' 'I heard the moth
Breed perilous worms.' 'I wept
All night, watching you rest.' 'I never slept
Nor sleep at all.' Thus ghastly they speak, both.

How can these sleep who eat upon their fear
And watch their dreadful love fade as it grows?
Their life flowers like an antique lovers' rose
Set puff'd and spreading in the chemist's jar.

I am your son, and from bad dreams arise.
My sight is fixed with horror, as I pass
Before the transitory glass
And watch the fungus cover up my eyes.

In 1929

A whim of Time, the general arbiter,
Proclaims the love, instead of death, of friends.
Under the domed sky and athletic sun
Three stand naked: the new, bronzed German,
The communist clerk, and myself, being English.

Yet to unwind the travelled sphere twelve years
Then two take arms, spring to a ghostly posture.
Or else roll on the thing a further ten
And this poor clerk with world-offended eyes
Builds with red hands his heaven; makes our
    bones
The necessary scaffolding to peace.

*   *   *

Now I suppose that the once-envious dead
Have learnt a strict philosophy of clay
After these centuries, to haunt us no longer
In the churchyard or at the end of the lane
Or howling at the edge of the city
Beyond the last beanrows, near the new factory.

Our fathers killed. And yet there lives no feud
Like Hamlet prompted on the castle stair;
There falls no shade across our blank of peace
We being together, struck across our path,
Nor taper finger threatening solitude.

Our fathers' misery, the ghost's mercy,
The cynic's mystery, weave this philosophy:
That the history of man, traced purely from
    dust,
Is lipping skulls on the revolving rim
Or posture of genius with the granite head bowed:

Lives risen a moment, joined or separate,
Fall heavily, then are always separate,
Stratum unreckoned by geologists,
Sod lifted, turned, slapped back again with spade.

The Shadow of a War

Who live under the shadow of a war,
What can I do that matters?
My pen stops, and my laughter, dancing, stop,
Or ride to a gap.

How often, on the powerful crest of pride,
I am shot with thought
That halts the untamed horses of the blood,
The grip on good;

That moving, whimpering, and mating, bear
Tunes to deaf ears:
Stuffed with the realer passions of the earth
Beneath this hearth.

Remembering

(*To* T.A.R.H.)

Even whilst I watch him I am remembering
The quick laugh of the wasp-gold eyes.
The column turning from the staring window
Even while I see I remember, for love
Dips what it sees into an endless present
That stays always the moment seeing
Of the once seen. Thus what I wore I wear
And shall wear always — the glint of the quick lids
And the body's axle turning: these shall be
   What they are now within my narrow Ever.

Night when my life lies with no past or future
But the room's little space. It wakes and watches
Hope and despair and the small vivid longings
Gnaw the flesh, like minnows. Where it drank love
It breathes in sameness. Here are
The signs indelible. The wiry copper hair,
And the notched mothlike lips, and that after all human
Glance, which makes all else forgiven.

The Prisoners

Far far the least of all, in want,
Are these,
The prisoners
Turned massive with their vaults and dark with dark.

They raise no hands, which rest upon their knees,
But lean their solid eyes against the night,
Dimly they feel
Only the furniture they use in cells.

Their Time is almost Death. The silted flow
Of years on years
Is marked by dawns
As faint as cracks on mud-flats of despair.

My pity moves amongst them like a breeze
On walls of stone,
Fretting for summer leaves, or like a tune
On ears of stone.

Then, when I raise my hands to strike,
It is too late,
There are no chains that fall
Nor visionary liquid door
Melted with anger.

When have their lives been free from walls and dark
And airs that choke?
And where less prisoner, to let my anger
Like a sun strike?

If I could follow them from room to womb
To plant some hope
Through the black silk of the big-bellied gown,
There would I win.

No, no, no,
It is too late for anger,
Nothing prevails
But pity for the grief they cannot feel.

The Truly Great

I think continually of those who were truly great.
Who, from the womb, remembered the soul's history
Through corridors of light where the hours are suns,
Endless and singing. Whose lovely ambition
Was that their lips, still touched with fire,
Should tell of the Spirit, clothed from head to foot in song.
And who hoarded from the Spring branches
The desires falling across their bodies like blossoms.

What is precious, is never to forget
The essential delight of the blood drawn from ageless springs
Breaking through rocks in worlds before our earth.
Never to deny its pleasure in the morning simple light
Nor its grave evening demand for love.
Never to allow gradually the traffic to smother
With noise and fog, the flowering of the Spirit.

Near the snow, near the sun, in the highest fields,
See how these names are fêted by the waving grass
And by the streamers of white cloud
And whispers of wind in the listening sky.
The names of those who in their lives fought for life,
Who wore at their hearts the fire's centre.
Born of the sun, they travelled a short while toward the sun
And left the vivid air signed with their honour.

Perhaps

The explosion of a bomb
The submarine a burst bubble filled with water
And the mine flooded — an accident, I hope —

Chancellor Dollfuss clutching his shot arm
The Reichstag that their own side set on fire
And then Our Party banned

Motor-cycles wires aeroplanes cars trains
Converging on that town Geneva
Top-hats orating at edge of silk-blue lake
Beyond, the mountains

We know these from rotating machines
From flanges stamping, cutting, unrolling —
Newsmen are compass-points, their arms
The four winds bearing legends —
We, fish-heads wrapped in what they print.

*   *   *

In his skidding car King Alexander wondered
Watching bayoneted landscape rush towards him:
'Is it the enemy? (I cannot grasp it) or is it
At peace with its own nature I cannot touch?'

Was that final when they shot him? Did that war
Lop off dead branches? Are the blonde youths splendid?
Is that revolution the whale of the future
Nosing through ice on the Antarctic edge?

Only Perhaps. Maybe that we shrivel
Donnish and bony, shut in our racing tombs:
Headlines are walls that shake and close
The dry dice rattled in their box.

Maybe deception of things merely changing. Out there
Perhaps it is the ghosts above the plain
Who grow. Not time-bombs but all time,
Monstrous with stillness, yonder Alpine range.

Van der Lubbe

O staring eyes, searchlight disks,
Listen to my lips! Now I'm louder than to
Swim the channel, be your boy, climb
The city's tallest flagpole.

I throw you words, I don't care what —
You must eat up my scraps and dance.
I'm glad, I'm glad this people are mad
And the papers drink in my mad glance.

Why do you laugh? The hooded judge asks.
I laugh at this trial even though it will make
My life end at a dazzling steel gate,
Axe severing a stalk.

Yes, No. Yes. No. Shall I tell you what I know?
Not to Goering — dear microphone, I whisper it to you.
I laugh because my laughter
Is German justice, twisted to a howitzer.

The senses are shaken from the judging heart.
The eye turned backwards, and the outside world
Inside the grave of the skull rolled;
With no God riding heaven, and disparate.

Contempt of justice, the delight of mere guns
Exploding trees where in the green branches
Truth soberly balanced, are what I am
Who die with you all and spit at you for fun.

The Express

After the first powerful, plain manifesto
The black statement of pistons, without more fuss
But gliding like a queen, she leaves the station.
Without bowing and with restrained unconcern
She passes the houses which humbly crowd outside,
The gasworks, and at last the heavy page
Of death, printed by gravestones in the cemetery.
Beyond the town, there lies the open country
Where, gathering speed, she acquires mystery,
The luminous self-possession of ships on ocean.
It is now she begins to sing — at first quite low
Then loud, and at last with a jazzy madness —
The song of her whistle screaming at curves,
Of deafening tunnels, brakes, innumerable bolts.
And always light, aerial, underneath,
Retreats the elate metre of her wheels.
Steaming through metal landscape on her lines,
She plunges new eras of white happiness,
Where speed throws up strange shapes, broad curves
And parallels clean like trajectories from guns.
At last, further than Edinburgh or Rome,
Beyond the crest of the world, she reaches night
Where only a low stream-line brightness
Of phosphorus on the tossing hills is light.
Ah, like a comet through flame, she moves entranced,
Wrapt in her music no bird song, no, nor bough
Breaking with honey buds, shall ever equal.

The Landscape
near an Aerodrome

More beautiful and soft than any moth
With burring furred antennae feeling its huge path
Through dusk, the air liner with shut-off engines
Glides over suburbs and the sleeves set trailing tall
To point the wind. Gently, broadly, she falls,
Scarcely disturbing charted currents of air.

Lulled by descent, the travellers across sea
And across feminine land indulging its easy limbs
In miles of softness, now let their eyes trained by
    watching
Penetrate through dusk the outskirts of this town
Here where industry shows a fraying edge.
Here they may see what is being done.

Beyond the winking masthead light
And the landing ground, they observe the
    outposts
Of work: chimneys like lank black fingers
Or figures, frightening and mad: and squat buildings
With their strange air behind trees, like women's
    faces
Shattered by grief. Here where few houses
Moan with faint light behind their blinds,
They remark the unhomely sense of complaint, like a dog
Shut out, and shivering at the foreign moon.

In the last sweep of love, they pass over fields
Behind the aerodrome, where boys play all day
Hacking dead grass: whose cries, like wild birds,
Settle upon the nearest roofs
But soon are hid under the loud city.

Then, as they land, they hear the tolling bell
Reaching across the landscape of hysteria,
To where, louder than all those batteries
And charcoaled towers against that dying sky,
Religion stands, the Church blocking the sun.

The Pylons

The secret of these hills was stone, and cottages
Of that stone made,
And crumbling roads
That turned on sudden hidden villages.

Now over these small hills, they have built the concrete
That trails black wire;
Pylons, those pillars
Bare like nude giant girls that have no secret.

The valley with its gilt and evening look
And the green chestnut
Of customary root,
Are mocked dry like the parched bed of a brook.

But as far above and far as sight endures
Like whips of anger
With lightning's danger
There runs the quick perspective of the future.

This dwarfs our emerald country by its trek
So tall with prophecy:
Dreaming of cities
Where often clouds shall lean their swan-white neck.

Not Palaces

Not palaces, an era's crown
Where the mind dwells, intrigues, rests;
Architectural gold-leaved flower
From people ordered like a single mind,
I build. This only what I tell:
It is too late for rare accumulation,
For family pride, for beauty's filtered dusts;
I say, stamping the words with emphasis,
Drink from here energy and only energy,
As from the electric charge of a battery,
To will this Time's change.
Eye, gazelle, delicate wanderer,
Drinker of horizon's fluid line;
Ear that suspends on a chord
The spirit drinking timelessness;
Touch, love, all senses;
Leave your gardens, your singing feasts,
Your dreams of suns circling before our sun,
Of heaven after our world.
Instead, watch images of flashing glass
That strike the outward sense, the polished will,
Flag of our purpose which the wind engraves.
No spirit seek here rest. But this: No one
Shall hunger: Man shall spend equally.
Our goal which we compel: Man shall be man.

That programme of the antique Satan
Bristling with guns on the indented page,
With battleship towering from hilly waves:
For what? Drive of a ruining purpose
Destroying all but its age-long exploiters.
Our programme like this, but opposite,
Death to the killers, bringing light to life.

Part Two

1934-1939

Polar Exploration

Our single purpose was to walk through snow
With faces swung to their prodigious North
Like compass needles. As clerks in whited banks
Leave bird-claw pen-prints columned on white paper,
On snow we added footprints.
Extensive whiteness drowned
All sense of space. We tramped through
Static, glaring days, Time's suspended blank.
That was in Spring and Autumn. Summer struck
Water over rocks, and half the world
Became a ship with a deep keel, the booming floes
And icebergs with their little birds:
Twittering Snow Bunting, Greenland Wheatear,
Red-throated Divers. Imagine butterflies,
Sulphurous cloudy yellow; burnish of bees
That suck from saxifrage; crowberry,
Bilberry, cranberry, *Pyrola Uniflora*.
There followed winter in a frozen hut
Warm enough at the kernel, but dare to sleep
With head against the wall — ice gummed my hair!
Hate Culver's loud breathing, despise Freeman's
Fidget for washing: love only the dogs
That whine for scraps, and scratch. Notice
How they run better (on short journeys) with a bitch.
In that, different from us.

Return, return, you warn! We do. There is
Your city, with railways, money, words, words, words.
Meals, papers, exchanges, debates,
Cinema, wireless: then there is Marriage.
I cannot sleep. At night I watch
A clear voice speak with words like drawing.
Its questions are white rifts: Was
Ice, our rage transformed? The raw, the motionless
Skies, were these the Spirit's hunger?

The continual hypnotized march through snow,
The dropping nights of precious extinction, were these
Only the wide circuits of the will,
The frozen heart's evasions? If such thoughts seem
A kind of madness here, a coldness
Of snow like sheets in summer — is the North
Over there, a palpable, true madness,
A solid simplicity, absolute, without towns,
Only with bears and fish, a raging eye,
A new and singular sex?

An Elementary School Classroom in a Slum

Far far from gusty waves these children's faces.
Like rootless weeds, the hair torn round their pallor.
The tall girl with her weighed-down head. The paper-
    seeming boy, with rat's eyes. The stunted, unlucky heir
Of twisted bones, reciting a father's gnarled disease,
His lesson from his desk. At back of the dim class
One unnoted, sweet and young. His eyes live in a dream
Of squirrel's game, in tree room, other than this.

On sour cream walls, donations. Shakespeare's head,
Cloudless at dawn, civilized dome riding all cities.
Belled, flowery, Tyrolese valley. Open-handed map
Awarding the world its world. And yet, for these
Children, these windows, not this world, are world,
Where all their future's painted with a fog,
A narrow street sealed in with a lead sky,
Far far from rivers, capes, and stars of words.

Surely, Shakespeare is wicked, the map a bad example
With ships and sun and love tempting them to steal —
For lives that slyly turn in their cramped holes
From fog to endless night? On their slag heap, these children
Wear skins peeped through by bones and spectacles of steel
With mended glass, like bottle bits on stones.
All of their time and space are foggy slum.
So blot their maps with slums as big as doom.

Unless, governor, teacher, inspector, visitor,
This map becomes their window and these windows
That shut upon their lives like catacombs,
Break O break open till they break the town
And show the children to green fields, and make their world
Run azure on gold sands, and let their tongues
Run naked into books, the white and green leaves open
History theirs whose language is the sun.

A Footnote

(From Marx's Chapter, *The Working Day*)

'Heard say that four times four is eight,'
'And the King is the Man what has all the Gold.'
'Our King is a Queen and her son's a Princess
'And they live in a Palace called London, I'm told.'

'Heard say that a man called God who's a Dog
'Made the World, with us in it.' 'And then I've
    heard
'There came a great Flood and the World was all
    drownded
'Except for one Man, and he was a Bird.'

'So perhaps all the People are dead, and we're Birds
'Shut in steel cages by the Devil, who's good,
'Like the Miners in their pit cages
'And us in our Chimneys to climb, as we should.'

— Ah, twittering voices
Of children crawling on their knees
Through notes of Blue Books, History Books,
At foot of the most crowded pages,
You are the birds of a songless age
Young like the youngest gods, awarded
Mythical childhood always.
Stunted spirits in a fog
Weaving pits and mills
Into tapestries of smoke,
You whisper among wheels
Calling to your stripped and sacred mothers
With straps tied round their waists
For dragging trucks along a line.
In the sunset above London

Often I watch you leaning between clouds
Drawn back like two curtains —
O cupids and cherubim
Of an impervious insensate age.

The Room above the Square

The light in the window seemed perpetual
When you stayed in the high room for me;
It glowed above the trees through leaves
Like my certainty.

The light is fallen and you are hidden
In sunbright peninsulas of the sword:
Torn like leaves through Europe is the peace
That through us flowed.

Now I climb up alone to the high room
Above the darkened square
Where among stones and roots, the other
Unshattered lovers are.

Thoughts during an Air Raid

Of course, the entire effort is to put oneself
Outside the ordinary range
Of what are called statistics. A hundred are killed
In the outer suburbs. Well, one carries on.
So long as this thing 'I' is propped up on
The girdered bed which seems so like a hearse,
In the hotel bedroom with the wall-paper
Blowing smoke-wreaths of roses, one can ignore
The pressure of those names under the fingers
Indented by lead type on newsprint,
In the bar, the marginal wailing wireless.
Yet supposing that a bomb should dive
Its nose right through this bed, with one upon it?
The thought's obscene. Still, there are many
For whom one's loss would illustrate
The 'impersonal' use indeed. The essential is
That every 'one' should remain separate
Propped up under roses, and no one suffer
For his neighbour. Then horror is postponed
Piecemeal for each, until it settles on him
That wreath of incommunicable grief
Which is all mystery or nothing.

Ultima Ratio Regum

The guns spell money's ultimate reason
In letters of lead on the Spring hillside.
But the boy lying dead under the olive trees
Was too young and too silly
To have been notable to their important eye.
He was a better target for a kiss.

When he lived, tall factory hooters never summoned him
Nor did restaurant plate-glass doors revolve to wave him in
His name never appeared in the papers.
The world maintained its traditional wall
Round the dead with their gold sunk deep as a well,
Whilst his life, intangible as a Stock Exchange rumour, drifted
    outside.

O too lightly he threw down his cap
One day when the breeze threw petals from the trees.
The unflowering wall sprouted with guns,
Machine-gun anger quickly scythed the grasses;
Flags and leaves fell from hands and branches;
The tweed cap rotted in the nettles.

Consider his life which was valueless
In terms of employment, hotel ledgers, news files.
Consider. One bullet in ten thousand kills a man.
Ask. Was so much expenditure justified
On the death of one so young, and so silly
Lying under the olive trees, O world, O death?

A Stopwatch and an Ordnance Map

(*To* SAMUEL BARBER)

A stopwatch and an ordnance map.
At five a man fell to the ground
And the watch flew off his wrist
Like a moon struck from the earth
Marking a blank time that stares
On the tides of change beneath.
All under the olive trees.

A stopwatch and an ordnance map.
He stayed faithfully in that place
From his living comrade split
By dividers of the bullet
Opening wide the distances
Of his final loneliness.
All under the olive trees.

A stopwatch and an ordnance map.
And the bones are fixed at five
Under the moon's timelessness;
But another who lives on
Wears within his heart for ever
Space split open by the bullet.
All under the olive trees.

Part Three

1939–1947

The Flask of Tears

Tears pouring from her face of stone,
Angels from the heart, unhappiness
From some past when she slept alone —
Let me dry her eyes with these kisses.
I bear what comfort of commonplace
I can : torch on her coldness thrown.
And then we join in that caress
That drowns our need both to atone.

Stone face on which cold tears are wet,
There's something in me delicate
Reads through her eyes an ocean of green water.
And one by one the salty drops collects
Into an opalescent flask, reflects
The lost world weeping in its daughter.

Song

Stranger, you who hide my love
    In the curved cheek of a smile
And sleep with her upon a tongue
    Of soft lies that beguile,
        Your paradisal ecstasy
    Is justified is justified
By hunger of all beasts beneath
    The overhanging cloud
        Who to snatch quick pleasures run
        Before their momentary sun
Be eclipsed by death.

Lightly, lightly, from my sleep
    She stole, our vows of dew to break
Upon a day of melting rain
    Another love to take;
        Her happy happy perfidy
    Was justified was justified
Since compulsive needs of sense
    Clamour to be satisfied
        And she was never one to miss
        Plausible happiness
Of a new experience.

I, who stand beneath a bitter
    Blasted tree, with the green life
Of summer joy cut from my side
    By that self-justifying knife,
        In my exiled misery
    Were justified were justified
If upon two lives I preyed
    Or punished with my suicide,
        Or murdered pity in my heart
        Or two other lives did part
To make the world pay what I paid.

Oh, but supposing that I climb
    Alone to a high room of clouds
Up a ladder of the time
And lie upon a bed alone
    And tear a feather from a wing
And listen to the world below
And write round my high paper walls
    Anything and everything
Which I know and do not know!

The Double Shame

You must live through the time when everything hurts
When the space of the ripe, loaded afternoon
Expands to a landscape of white heat frozen
And trees are weighed down with hearts of stone
And green stares back where you stare alone,
And the walking eyes throw flinty comments,
And the words which carry most knives are the blind
Phrases searching to be kind.

Solid and usual objects are ghosts
The furniture carries cargoes of memory,
The staircase has corners which remember
As fire blows reddest in gusty embers,
And each empty dress cuts out an image
In fur and evening and summer and spring
Of her who was different in each.

Pull down the blind and lie on the bed
And clasp the hour in the glass of one room
Against your mouth like a crystal doom.
Take up the book and stare at the letters
Hieroglyphs on sand and as meaningless —
Here birds crossed once and a foot once trod
In a mist where sight and sound are blurred.

The story of others who made their mistakes
And of one whose happiness pierced like a star
Eludes and evades between sentences
And the letters break into eyes which read
The story life writes now in your head
As though the characters sought for some clue
To their being so poignantly living and dead
In your history, worse than theirs, but true.

Set in the mind of their poet, they compare
Their tragic sublime with your tawdry despair

And they have fingers which accuse
You of the double way of shame.
At first you did not love enough
And afterwards you loved too much
And you lacked the confidence to choose
And you have only yourself to blame.

The War God

Why cannot the one good
Benevolent feasible
Final dove, descend?

And the wheat be divided?
And the soldiers sent home?
And the barriers torn down?
And the enemies forgiven?
And there be no retribution?

Because the conqueror
Is the victim of his own power
Hammering his will
Out of fear of former fear:
Remembering yesterday
When those he now vanquishes
Destroyed his hero-father
And surrounded his cradle
With fabled anguishes.

Today his sun of victory
Hides the night's anxiety
Lest children of the slain
Prove dragon teeth sown
By their sun going down,
To rise up tomorrow
In sky and sea all blood
And avenge their fathers again.

Those who surrender
On the helpless field
May dream the pious reasons
Of mercy, but alas
They know what they did
In their own sun-high season.

For the world is the world
And not the slain
Nor the slayer forgive
And it writes no histories
That end in love.

Yet under the waves'
Chains chafing despair
Love's need does not cease.

Air Raid across the Bay at Plymouth

I

Above the whispering sea
And waiting rocks of black coast,
Across the bay, the searchlight beams
Swing and swing back across the sky.

　　Their ends fuse in a cone of light
Held for a bright instant up
Until they break away again
Smashing that image like a cup.

II

Delicate aluminium girders
Project phantom aerial masts
Swaying crane and derrick
Above the seas' just surging deck.

III

Triangles, parallels, parallelograms,
Experiment with hypotheses
On the blackboard sky,
Seeking that X
Where the raider is met.
Two beams cross
To chalk his cross.

IV

　　A sound, ragged, unseen
Is pursued by swords of light.
　　A thud. An instant when the whole night gleams.
Gold sequins shake out of a black-silk screen.

V

Jacob ladders slant
Up to the god of war
Who, from his heaven-high car,
Unloads upon a star
A destroying star.

Round the coast, the waves
Chuckle between rocks.
In the fields the corn
Sways, with metallic clicks.
Man hammers nails in Man,
Upon his crucifix.

A Man-made World

What a wild room
We enter, when the gloom
Of windowless night
Shuts us from the light

In a black malicious box.
Then a key locks
Us into the utter dark
Where the nerves hark

For the man-made toys
To whirr, unwinding noise.
The siren wails. After,
Broomsticks climb air,

Clocks break their springs,
Then the fire bell rings.
From high and low comes,
The thunder of the drums.

Ah, what white rays gleaming
Up to the sky's low ceiling!
Ah, what flashes show
A woman who cries: 'Oh!'

Thus the world we made
Pays back what we paid;
Thus the dark descends.
Our means became our ends.

Memento

Remember the blackness of that flesh
Tarring the bones with a thin varnish
Belsen Theresenstadt Buchenwald where
Faces were a clenched despair
Knocking at the bird-song-fretted air.

Their eyes sunk jellied in their holes
Were held up to the sun like begging bowls
Their hands like rakes with finger-nails of rust
Scratched for a little kindness from the dust.
To many, in its beak, no dove brought answer.

Epilogue to a Human Drama

When pavements were blown up, exposing nerves,
And the gas mains burned blue and gold,
And stucco and brick were pulverized to a cloud
Pungent with smells of mice, dust, garlic, anxiety:
When the reverberant emptied façades
Of the West End palaces of commerce
Isolated in a vacuum of silence, suddenly
Cracked and blazed and fell, with the seven-maned
Lions of Wrath licking the stony fragments —

Then the one voice through deserted streets
Was the Cassandra bell which rang and rang and ran
Released at last by Time
To seek those fires that burst through many walls —
Prophecies come true under our nostrils,
Blood and fire streaming from the stones.

London burned with unsentimental dignity
Of resigned kingship: those stores and Churches
Which had glittered century-long in tarnished gold
Stood near the throne of domed St. Paul's
Like courtiers round the Royal sainted martyr.
August shadows of night
And bursting shells of concentrated light
Dropped from the skies to paint a final scene
Illuminated agony of frowning stone.
Who can wonder then that every word
In burning London, stepped out of a play?

On the stage, there were heroes, maidens, fools,
Victims, a Chorus. The heroes were brave,
The fools spat jokes into the skull of death,

The victims waited with the humble patience
Of animals trapped behind a wall
For the pickaxes to break, with light and water.
The Chorus assisted, bringing cups of tea.

from Explorations

Within our nakedness, nakedness still
Is the naked mind. Past and stars show
Through the columned bones. Tomorrow
Will blow away the temple of each will.
The Universe, by inches, minutes, fills
Our hollowed tongues. Name and image glow
In word, in form. Star and history know
That they exist, in life existence kills.

    Revolving on the earth rim through the night,
Homunculi, pulsing blood and breath,
Separate in separation, yet unite
For that last journey to no place nor date,
Where, naked beneath nakedness, beneath
Each, all are nothing, who await
The multitudinous loneliness of death.

*   *   *

Since we are what we are, what shall we be
But what we are? We are, we have
Six feet and seventy years, to see
The light, and then resign it for the grave.
We are not worlds, no, nor infinity,
We have no claims on stone, except to prove
In the invention of the human city
Ourselves, our breath, our death, our love.

    The tower we build soars like an arrow
From the earth's rim towards the sky's,
Upwards-downwards in a star-filled pond,
Climbing and diving from our Earth to narrow
The gap between the world shut in the eyes
And the receding world of light beyond.

*   *   *

One is the witness through whom the whole
Knows it exists. Within his coils of blood,
Drumming under his sleep, there moves the flood
Of stars, battles, dark and glacial pole.
One is all that one is not. On his dreams ride
Dead ancestors. All spaces outside
Glitter under his ribs. Being all things, one is one.
    I who say I call that eye I
Which is the mirror in which things see
Nothing except themselves. I die.
The world, the things seen, still will be.
Upon this eye the vast reflections lie
But that which passes, passes away, is I.

Daybreak

At dawn she lay with her profile at that angle
Which, when she sleeps, seems the carved face of an angel.
Her hair a harp, the hand of a breeze follows
And plays, against the white cloud of the pillows.
Then, in a flush of rose, she woke, and her eyes that opened
Swam in blue through her rose flesh that dawned.
From her dew of lips, the drop of one word
Fell like the first of fountains: murmured
'Darling', upon my ears the song of the first bird.
'My dream becomes my dream,' she said, 'come true.
I waken from you to my dream of you.'
Oh, my own wakened dream then dared assume
The audacity of her sleep. Our dreams
Poured into each other's arms, like streams.

Seascape

(*In Memoriam*, M.A.S.)

There are some days, the happy ocean lies
Like an unfingered harp, below the land.
Afternoon gilds all the silent wires
Into a burning music for the eyes.
On mirrors dangled between thin-stretched fires
The shore, heaped up with roses, horses, spires,
Walks over water, through which is seen ribbed sand.

Motionlessness of the hot sky tires,
And a sigh, like a woman's, from inland,
Brushes the instrument with shading hand
Drawing across those wires some gull's sharp cries
Or bell, or shout, from distant, hedged-in shires:
These, deep as anchors, the hushing wave buries.

Then, from the shore, two zig-zag butterflies,
Like errant dog-roses, cross the gold strand
Spiralling in besotted gyres
Until they fall in sea-reflecting skies.
They drown. Fishermen understand
Such wings sunk in such ritual sacrifice,

Recalling legends of undersea, drowned cities.
What voyagers, heroes, falling stars and pyres
With helmets plumed, have set forth from some island
And them the sea engulfed! Their eyes,
Distorted by the cruel waves' desires
Glitter with coins, through the tide scarcely scanned,
While, above them, that harp assumes their sighs.

The Barn

Half hidden by trees, the sheer roof of the barn
Is a river of tiles, warped
By winding currents of weather
Suns and storms ago.

Through beech leaves, its vermilion shows
A Red Admiral's wing, with veins
Of lichen and rust, an underwing
Of winter-reft leaves.

Now, in the Spring, a sapling's jet
Of new, gold green, cuts across
The low lead gutter. Twin leaves hold up
Red tiles reflected in their cup.

At the side of the road where cars crash past,
The barn lies under the sky — a throat
Full of dark gurgitation:

A ghost of a noise, a hint of a gust
Caught in the rafters centuries ago:
The creak of a winch, the wood of a wheel.

Entangled in murmurs, as in a girl's hair,
Is the enthusiastic scent
Of hysterical straw — caught by that sunbeam
Which, laden with motes, strikes across the floor.

Part Four

LATER POEMS

The Trance

Sometimes, apart in sleep, by chance,
You fall out of my arms, alone,
Into the chaos of your separate trance.
My eyes gaze through your forehead, through the bone,
And see where in your sleep distress has torn
Its path, which on your lips is shown
And on your hands and in your dream forlorn.

Restless, you turn to me, and press
Those timid words against my ear
Which thunder at my heart like stones.
'Mercy,' you plead, Then 'Who can bless?'
You ask. 'I am pursued by Time,' you moan.
I watch that precipice of fear
You tread, naked in naked distress.

To that deep care we are committed
Beneath the wildness of our flesh
And shuddering horror of our dream,
Where unmasked agony is permitted.
Our bodies, stripped of clothes that seem,
And our souls, stripped of beauty's mesh,
Meet their true selves, their charms outwitted.

This pure trance is the oracle
That speaks no language but the heart,
Our angel with our devil meets
In the atrocious dark nor do they part
But each each forgives and greets,
And their mutual terrors heal
Within our married miracle.

Word

The word bites like a fish.
Shall I throw it back free
Arrowing to that sea
Where thoughts lash tail and fin?
Or shall I pull it in
To rhyme upon a dish?

In Attica

Again, again, I see this form repeated:
The bare shadow of a rock outlined
Against the sky; declining gently to
An elbow; then the scooped descent
From the elbow to the wrist of a hand that rests
On the plain.
                    Again, again,
That arm outstretched from the high shoulder
And leaning on the land.
                              As though the torsoed
Gods, with heads and lower limbs broken off,
Plunged in the sky, or buried under earth,
Had left fingers here as pointers
Between the sun and plain:
                                    had made this landscape
Human, like Greek steles, where the dying
Are changed to stone on a gesture of curved air,
Lingering in their infinite departure.

To my Daughter

Bright clasp of her whole hand around my finger,
My daughter, as we walk together now.
All my life I'll feel a ring invisibly
Circle this bone with shining: when she is grown
Far from today as her eyes are far already.

Nocturne

Their six-weeks-old daughter lies
  in her cot, crying out the night. Their hearts
Are sprung like armies, waiting
To cross the gap to where her loneliness
Lies infinite between them. This child's cry
Sends rays of a star's pain through endless dark;
And the sole purpose of their loving
Is to disprove her demonstration
Of all love's aidlessness. Words unspoken
Out of her mouth unsaying, prove unhappiness
Pure as innocence, virgin of tragedy,
Unknowing reason. Star on star of pain
Surround her cry to make a constellation
Where human tears of victims are the same
As griefs of the unconscious animals.

  Listening, the parents know this primal cry
Out of the gates of life, hollows such emptiness,
It proves that all men's aims should be, all times,
To fill the gap of pain with consolation
Poured from the mountain-sided adult lives
Whose minds like peaks attain to heights of snow:
The snow should stoop to wash away such grief.
Unceasing love should lave the feet of victims.

  Yet, when they lift their heads out of such truths,
Today mocks at their prayers. To think this even
Suffices to remind them of far worse
Man-made man-destroying ills which threaten
While they try to lull a child. For she
Who cries for milk, for rocking, and a shawl,
Is also subject to the rage of causes
Dividing peoples. Even at this moment
Eyes might fly between them and the moon,
And a hand touch a lever to let fall

That which would make the street of begging roofs
Pulverize and creep skywards in a tower:
Down would fall baby, cradle, and them all.

That which sent out the pilot to destroy them
Was the same will as that with which they send
An enemy to kill their enemy. Even in this love
Running in shoals on each side of her bed,
Is fear, and hate. If they shift their glances
From her who weeps, their eyes meet other eyes
Willed with death, also theirs. All would destroy
New-born, innocent streets. Necessity,
With abstract head and searing feet, men's god
Unseeing the poor amulets of flesh,
Unhearing the minutiae of prayer.

Parents like mountains watching above their child,
Envallied here beneath them, also hold
Upon their frozen heights, the will that sends
Destruction into centres of the stones
Which concentrated locked centennial stillness
For human generations to indwell.

Hearing their daughter's cry which is the speech
Of indistinguishable primal life,
They know the dark is filled with means which are
Men's plots to murder children. They know too
No cause is just unless it guards the innocent
As sacred trust: no truth but that
Which reckons this child's tears an argument.

Subject: Object: Sentence

A subject thought: because he had a verb
With several objects, that he ruled a sentence.
Had not the Grammar willed him these substantives
Which he came into, as his just inheritance?

His objects were *wine, women, fame* and *wealth,*
And a subordinate clause — *all life can give.*
He grew so fond of having these that, finally,
He found himself becoming quite subjective.

Subject, the dictionary warned means *someone ruled by*
Person or thing. Was he not *having*'s slave?
To achieve detachment, he must be *objective*
Which meant to free himself from the verb *have.*

Seeking detachment, he studied the context
Around his sentence, to place it in perspective:
Paraphrased, made a critical analysis,
And then re-read it, feeling more *objective.*

Then, with a shock, he realized that *sentence*
Like *subject-object* is treacherously double.
A sentence is condemned to stay as stated —
As in *life-sentence, death-sentence,* for example.

'Earth-treading stars that make dark heaven light'

How can they call this dark when stars
That all day long the sun rules out
Show brilliant at the ends of space?
Journeying down centennial rays
These antique worlds stand in Earth's air —
The coruscating helmets of
Warriors born before the births
Of Greeks who chose their diamond names.

All day the sun paints surfaces,
Commander of dial hands, pursues
The flying instants of last fashion.
But when night comes and windows hew
Gold oblongs out of distances
Of solid sky, the park becomes
The fulgurous centre of the city
Drawing from lonely streets the lonely

Under its boughs. There, in each other,
Beyond their coverings of clothes
And names, they see flesh blaze, and then
Those pasts they were before they were
Themselves, emerge : ape, lion, fox. Their mouths
Conjoined, they utter cries that once
Jibbered upside down through branches
Before woods ever dreamed of huts.

But two there are who look so deep
Into each other's night, they see
Yet further than their meeting bodies
And earliest most brilliant star,
To where is nothing but a vow
That is their truth. Those instruments
Of world made flesh, they bore to prove
Before all change, their changeless word.

One More New Botched Beginning

Their voices heard, I stumble suddenly,
Choking in undergrowth. I'm torn
Mouth pressed against the thorns,
                                    remembering
        Ten years ago here in Geneva,

I walked with Merleau-Ponty by the lake.
Upon his face I saw his intellect.
The energy of the sun-interweaving
Waves, electric, danced on him. His eyes
Smiled with their gay logic through
Black coins thrown down from leaves. He who
Was Merleau-Ponty that day is no more
Irrevocable than the I that day who was
Beside him — I'm still living!

        Also that summer
My son stayed up the valley in the mountains.
One day I went to see him, and he stood
Not seeing me, watching some hens.
Doing so, he was absorbed
In their wire-netted world. He danced
On one leg. Leaning forward, he became
A bird-boy. I am there
Still seeing him. To him
That moment — unselfknowing even then —
Is drowned in the oblivious earliness . . .
                                    Such pasts

Are not diminished distances, perspective
Vanishing points, but doors
Burst open suddenly by gusts
That seek to blow the heart out . . .
                                    Today, I see
Three undergraduates standing talking in
A college quad. They show each other poems —
Louis MacNeice, Bernard Spencer, and I.

Louis caught cold in the rain, Bernard fell
From a train door.

Their lives are now those poems that were
Pointers to the poems to be their lives.
We read there in the college quad, each poem
Is still a new beginning. If
They had been finished though, they would have died
Before they died. Being alive
Is when each moment's a new start, with past
And future shuffled between fingers
For a new game. I'm dealing out
My hand to them, one more new botched beginning
There, where we still stand talking in the quad.